# THANK YOU, GOD!

## a Jewish child's book of prayers

*Judyth Groner and Madeline Wikler*
*illustrated by Shelly O. Haas*

KAR-BEN COPIES, INC. • ROCKVILLE, MD

*For our mothers,*
*Shirley Robbins*
*Fay Meyers*
*May their memory be for a blessing.*
*—JG & MW*


*To Faith from the heart capable of enduring*
*and enriching all life experiences • SOH*
*With special thanks to my two ''Ethels''*


## TRANSLITERATION HINTS

Because transliteration is phonetic, spellings can vary. In this book, sounds are represented as follows:

| | | | |
|---|---|---|---|
| *a* | as in bar | *o* | as in for |
| *ai* | as in aisle | *u* | as in rule |
| *e* | as in bet | *ch* | as in Bach |
| *ei* | as in rein | *g* | as in go |
| *i* | as in magazine | | |

An apostrophe between vowels indicates each vowel is pronounced separately.
Other apostrophes designate a vocalized pause.

Library of Congress Cataloging-in-Publication Data

Groner, Judyth Saypol.  Thank you, God!: a Jewish child's book of prayer/Judyth Groner and Madeline Wikler: illustrated by Shelly O. Haas. Summary: Presents common Jewish prayers and blessings in English and Hebrew with simple transliterations.  ISBN 0-929371-65-8:  1.  Jewish children—Prayer-books and devotions.  2.  Benedictions—Texts.  3.  Judaism—Liturgy—Texts. [1. Judaism—Liturgy.  2. Judaism—Prayer books and devotions.  3. Prayer books and devotions.]  I. Wikler, Madeline.  II. Haas, Shelly O., ill.  III. Title.  BM666.G76  1993  296.7'2—dc20  93-7550  CIP  AC

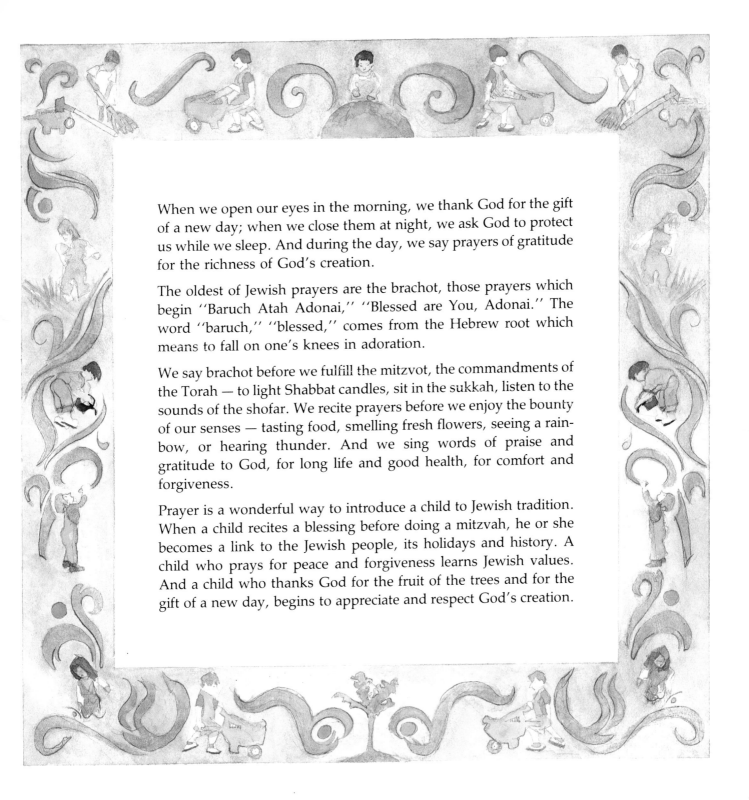

When we open our eyes in the morning, we thank God for the gift of a new day; when we close them at night, we ask God to protect us while we sleep. And during the day, we say prayers of gratitude for the richness of God's creation.

The oldest of Jewish prayers are the brachot, those prayers which begin "Baruch Atah Adonai," "Blessed are You, Adonai." The word "baruch," "blessed," comes from the Hebrew root which means to fall on one's knees in adoration.

We say brachot before we fulfill the mitzvot, the commandments of the Torah — to light Shabbat candles, sit in the sukkah, listen to the sounds of the shofar. We recite prayers before we enjoy the bounty of our senses — tasting food, smelling fresh flowers, seeing a rainbow, or hearing thunder. And we sing words of praise and gratitude to God, for long life and good health, for comfort and forgiveness.

Prayer is a wonderful way to introduce a child to Jewish tradition. When a child recites a blessing before doing a mitzvah, he or she becomes a link to the Jewish people, its holidays and history. A child who prays for peace and forgiveness learns Jewish values. And a child who thanks God for the fruit of the trees and for the gift of a new day, begins to appreciate and respect God's creation.

# GOOD MORNING

Each morning we awaken and give thanks
for the gift of a new day.

מוֹדֶה אֲנִי לְפָנֶיךָ, מֶלֶךְ חַי וְקַיָּם
שֶׁהֶחֱזַרְתָּ בִּי נִשְׁמָתִי בְּחֶמְלָה, רַבָּה אֱמוּנָתֶךָ.

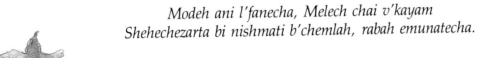

*Modeh ani l'fanecha, Melech chai v'kayam*
*Shehechezarta bi nishmati b'chemlah, rabah emunatecha.*

Thank You, God, for a good night's sleep
and a fresh chance to learn and grow.

# THE SH'MA

Every morning and every night
when we say the Sh'ma, we are saying,
''God is everywhere and God is One.''

שְׁמַע יִשְׂרָאֵל יְיָ אֱלֹהֵינוּ יְיָ אֶחָד.

*Sh'ma Yisra'el Adonai Eloheinu Adonai Echad.*

Listen, O Israel, Adonai is our God, Adonai Alone.
Blessed is Adonai Who rules forever.

וְאָהַבְתָּ אֵת יְיָ אֱלֹהֶיךָ בְּכָל־לְבָבְךָ
וּבְכָל־נַפְשְׁךָ וּבְכָל־מְאֹדֶךָ.

*V'ahavta et Adonai Elohecha b'chol l'vavcha*
*uv'chol nafsh'cha uv'chol m'odecha.*

We will love God with all our heart,
and all our might.
Now and in the future, at home and away,
from morning until night,
God's words will guide how we live.

# BEFORE A MEAL

Before we eat, we give thanks for our food.

בָּרוּךְ אַתָּה יְיָ אֱלֹהֵינוּ מֶלֶךְ הָעוֹלָם,
הַמּוֹצִיא לֶחֶם מִן הָאָרֶץ.

*Baruch Atah Adonai Eloheinu Melech ha'olam,
hamotzi lechem min ha'aretz.*

Thank You, God, for the blessing of bread
and for the meal we will now enjoy together.

# AFTER A MEAL

We join in giving thanks for the meal we have eaten.

בָּרוּךְ אַתָּה יְיָ, הַזָּן אֶת־הַכֹּל.

*Baruch Atah Adonai, hazan et hakol.*

Thank You, God, Who provides our food.
Help us to share what we have,
and to care for those who are hungry.

# OVER THE SHABBAT CANDLES

Come, let us welcome Shabbat.

בָּרוּךְ אַתָּה יְיָ אֱלֹהֵינוּ מֶלֶךְ הָעוֹלָם,
אֲשֶׁר קִדְּשָׁנוּ בְּמִצְוֹתָיו, וְצִוָּנוּ לְהַדְלִיק נֵר שֶׁל שַׁבָּת.

*Baruch Atah Adonai Eloheinu Melech ha'olam,*
*Asher kid'shanu b'mitzvotav, v'tzivanu l'hadlik ner shel Shabbat.*

Thank You, God, for the mitzvah of lighting the candles. May they shine upon us in love and peace.

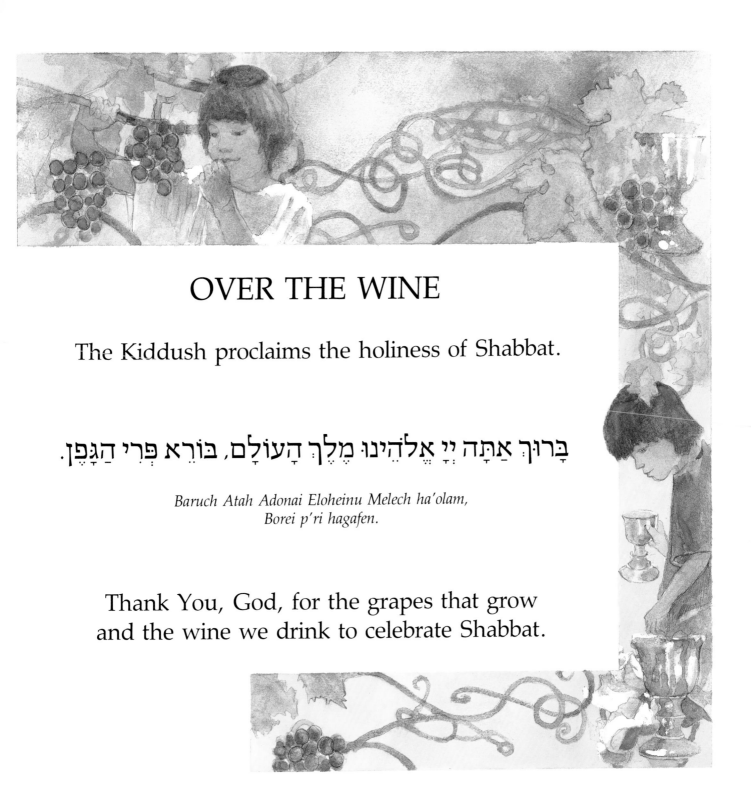

# OVER THE WINE

The Kiddush proclaims the holiness of Shabbat.

בָּרוּךְ אַתָּה יְיָ אֱלֹהֵינוּ מֶלֶךְ הָעוֹלָם, בּוֹרֵא פְּרִי הַגָּפֶן.

*Baruch Atah Adonai Eloheinu Melech ha'olam,*
*Borei p'ri hagafen.*

Thank You, God, for the grapes that grow
and the wine we drink to celebrate Shabbat.

# HAVDALAH

At Havdalah, we say good-bye to Shabbat
and welcome a new week.

בָּרוּךְ אַתָּה יְיָ
אֱלֹהֵינוּ מֶלֶךְ הָעוֹלָם,
בּוֹרֵא פְּרִי הַגָּפֶן.

*Baruch Atah Adonai*
*Eloheinu Melech ha'olam,*
*Borei p'ri hagafen.*

בָּרוּךְ אַתָּה יְיָ
אֱלֹהֵינוּ מֶלֶךְ הָעוֹלָם,
בּוֹרֵא מִינֵי בְשָׂמִים.

*Baruch Atah Adonai*
*Eloheinu Melech ha'olam,*
*Borei minei v'samim.*

Thank You, God,
for the fruit of the vine.

Thank You, God,
for fragrant spices.

בָּרוּךְ אַתָּה יְיָ
הַמַּבְדִּיל בֵּין קֹדֶשׁ לְחוֹל.

*Baruch Atah Adonai*
*Hamavdil bein kodesh l'chol.*

Thank You, God,
for making Shabbat
different from the
rest of the week.

בָּרוּךְ אַתָּה יְיָ
אֱלֹהֵינוּ מֶלֶךְ הָעוֹלָם,
בּוֹרֵא מְאוֹרֵי הָאֵשׁ.

*Baruch Atah Adonai*
*Eloheinu Melech ha'olam,*
*Borei m'orei ha'esh.*

Thank You, God,
for creating light.

# FOR A SWEET NEW YEAR

We welcome Rosh Hashanah with apples dipped in honey.

בָּרוּךְ אַתָּה יְיָ אֱלֹהֵינוּ מֶלֶךְ הָעוֹלָם, בּוֹרֵא פְּרִי הָעֵץ.

*Baruch Atah Adonai Eloheinu Melech ha'olam, borei p'ri ha'etz.*

Thank You, God, for the fruit of the trees.
We pray that the new year will be
a sweet and happy one for all.

# A YOM KIPPUR PRAYER

On Yom Kippur, we look back
and think about the past year.
Some things we did make us proud.
Other things make us sorry.

וְעַל כֻּלָם, אֱלוֹהַּ סְלִיחוֹת,
סְלַח לָנוּ, מְחַל־לָנוּ, כַּפֶּר־לָנוּ.

*V'al kulam, Elo'ah s'lichot,
S'lach lanu, m'chal lanu, kaper lanu.*

God, help us make up
for our mistakes.
Help us to forgive others
when they say they are sorry.
Forgive us, pardon us,
give us another chance.

# IN THE SUKKAH

When we sit in the sukkah we remember
the booths the Jews built in the desert
after they were freed from slavery in Egypt.

בָּרוּךְ אַתָּה יְיָ אֱלֹהֵינוּ מֶלֶךְ הָעוֹלָם,
אֲשֶׁר קִדְּשָׁנוּ בְּמִצְוֹתָיו, וְצִוָּנוּ לֵישֵׁב בַּסֻּכָּה.

*Baruch Atah Adonai Eloheinu Melech ha'olam,*
*Asher kid'shanu b'mitzvotav, v'tzivanu leishev basukkah.*

Thank You, God, for the mitzvah of sitting
in the sukkah with family and friends.

# LULAV AND ETROG

We shake the lulav and etrog in all directions
to show that God is everywhere.

בָּרוּךְ אַתָּה יְיָ אֱלֹהֵינוּ מֶלֶךְ הָעוֹלָם,
אֲשֶׁר קִדְּשָׁנוּ בְּמִצְוֹתָיו, וְצִוָּנוּ עַל־נְטִילַת לוּלָב.

*Baruch Atah Adonai Eloheinu Melech ha'olam,*
*Asher kid'shanu b'mitzvotav, v'tzivanu al n'tilat lulav.*

Thank You, God, for the harvest fruits and for
the sun and rain which make them grow.

# ON CHANUKAH

Each night of Chanukah we light another candle
to remember the victory of the brave Maccabees,
and the little jug of oil that burned for eight days.

בָּרוּךְ אַתָּה יְיָ אֱלֹהֵינוּ מֶלֶךְ הָעוֹלָם,
אֲשֶׁר קִדְּשָׁנוּ בְּמִצְוֹתָיו, וְצִוָּנוּ.
לְהַדְלִיק נֵר שֶׁל חֲנֻכָּה.

*Baruch Atah Adonai Eloheinu Melech ha'olam,*
*Asher kid'shanu b'mitzvotav, v'tzivanu l'hadlik ner shel Chanukah.*

Thank You, God, for the mitzvah of the Chanukah lights.
May they spark within us the courage to speak out for freedom.

בָּרוּךְ אַתָּה יְיָ אֱלֹהֵינוּ מֶלֶךְ הָעוֹלָם,
שֶׁעָשָׂה נִסִּים לַאֲבוֹתֵינוּ בַּיָּמִים הָהֵם בַּזְּמַן הַזֶּה.

*Baruch Atah Adonai Eloheinu Melech ha'olam,*
*She'asah nisim la'avoteinu bayamim hahem baz'man hazeh.*

Thank You, God, for the miracles which
saved our people, then and now.

*On the first night:*

בָּרוּךְ אַתָּה יְיָ
אֱלֹהֵינוּ מֶלֶךְ הָעוֹלָם,
שֶׁהֶחֱיָנוּ וְקִיְּמָנוּ
וְהִגִּיעָנוּ לַזְּמַן הַזֶּה.

*Baruch Atah Adonai*
*Eloheinu Melech ha'olam*
*Shehecheyanu v'kiy'manu,*
*V'higi'anu laz'man hazeh.*

Thank You, God,
for bringing us together
at this happy time.

# THE WONDERS OF NATURE

When we see a glowing sunset, a towering mountain, or a powerful stroke of lightning, we are reminded of God's creative power.

בָּרוּךְ אַתָּה יְיָ אֱלֹהֵינוּ מֶלֶךְ הָעוֹלָם,
עֹשֶׂה מַעֲשֵׂה בְרֵאשִׁית.

*Baruch Atah Adonai Eloheinu Melech ha'olam,*
*Oseh ma'aseh v'reishit.*

Thank You, God, for the world You have created. Help us to protect and preserve it for future generations.

# ON SEEING TREES BLOOM

When we see trees begin to bloom in spring, we
rejoice in the beauty of nature.

בָּרוּךְ אַתָּה יְיָ אֱלֹהֵינוּ
מֶלֶךְ הָעוֹלָם, שֶׁבָּרָא בּוֹ
בְּרִיּוֹת טוֹבוֹת וְאִילָנוֹת טוֹבִים
לְהַנּוֹת בָּהֶם בְּנֵי אָדָם.

*Baruch Atah Adonai*
*Eloheinu Melech ha'olam,*
*Shevara vo b'riyot tovot v'ilanot tovim*
*L'hanot bahem b'nei adam.*

Thank You, God, for creating beautiful creatures
and goodly trees, so we may enjoy them.

# FOR GOOD HEALTH

When someone is sick, we pray that they will get well.

מִי שֶׁבֵּרַךְ אֲבוֹתֵינוּ וְאִמּוֹתֵינוּ, אָנָּא רְפָא נָא אֶת־הַחוֹלִים.

*Mi sheberach avoteinu v'imoteinu, ana r'fa na et hacholim.*

May God Who has blessed
our fathers and our mothers,
heal those who are sick,
strengthen those who are weak,
and comfort those who suffer pain.

# ESCAPING DANGER

When we escape danger or recover from illness, we are grateful.

בָּרוּךְ אַתָּה יְיָ אֱלֹהֵינוּ מֶלֶךְ הָעוֹלָם, שֶׁגְּמָלַנִי כָּל־טוֹב.

*Baruch Atah Adonai Eloheinu Melech ha'olam, sheg'malani kol tov.*

Thank You, God, for Your comfort in my time of fear
and Your kindness in my time of need.

# MOURNER'S PRAYER

When we remember those who have died,
we think about the happy times we shared,
and the many things they taught us.

יְהֵא שְׁמֵהּ רַבָּא מְבָרַךְ
לְעָלַם וּלְעָלְמֵי עָלְמַיָּא.

*Yehei sh'mei raba m'varach*
*L'olam ul'almei almaya.*

Thank You, God, for the time we had together.
May Your name be praised forever and ever.

# FOR PEACE

We pray for peace in many ways.

עֹשֶׂה שָׁלוֹם בִּמְרוֹמָיו,
הוּא יַעֲשֶׂה שָׁלוֹם עָלֵינוּ,
וְעַל־כָּל־יִשְׂרָאֵל, וְאִמְרוּ אָמֵן.

*Oseh shalom bimromov,*
*Hu ya'aseh shalom aleinu,*
*V'al kol Yisra'el, v'imru amen.*

Grant us peace, O God.
Peace among the countries of the world.
Peace with our neighbors and friends.
Peace for our home and our family.
Peace with ourselves.

# GOOD NIGHT

As the day ends and the shadows of night fall,
we pray that our sleep is peaceful,
filled with pleasant dreams.
May we awaken rested and ready for a new day.

הַשְׁכִּיבֵנוּ יְיָ אֱלֹהֵינוּ לְשָׁלוֹם.

*Hashkivenu Adonai Eloheinu l'shalom.*

Thank You, God, for the day and its work
and the night and its rest.


שְׁמַע יִשְׂרָאֵל יְיָ אֱלֹהֵינוּ יְיָ אֶחָד.

*Sh'ma Yisra'el Adonai Eloheinu Adonai Echad.*

Listen, O Israel, Adonai is our God, Adonai Alone.

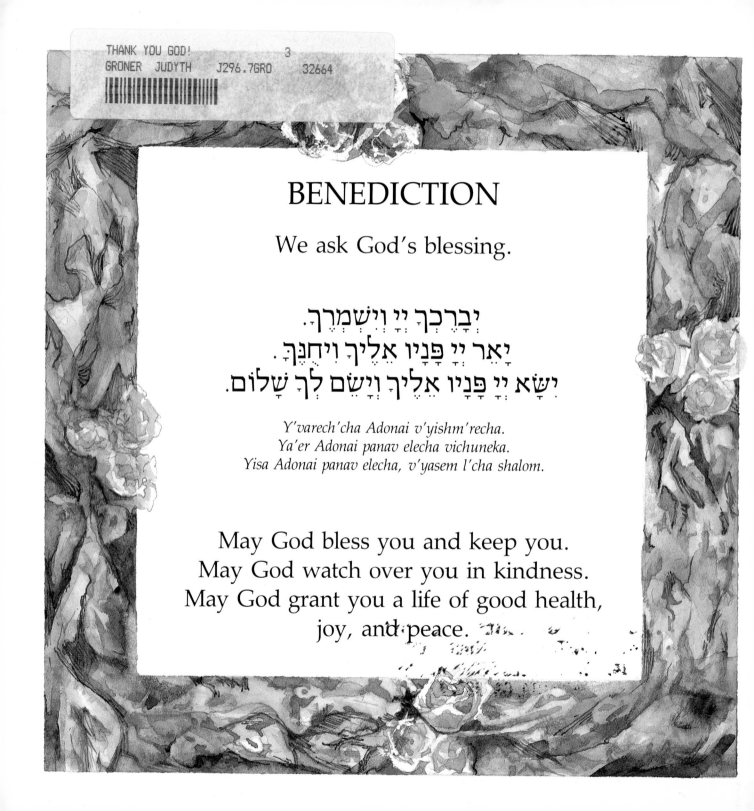

# BENEDICTION

We ask God's blessing.

יְבָרֶכְךָ יְיָ וְיִשְׁמְרֶךָ.

יָאֵר יְיָ פָּנָיו אֵלֶיךָ וִיחֻנֶּךָּ.

יִשָּׂא יְיָ פָּנָיו אֵלֶיךָ וְיָשֵׂם לְךָ שָׁלוֹם.

*Y'varech'cha Adonai v'yishm'recha.*
*Ya'er Adonai panav elecha vichuneka.*
*Yisa Adonai panav elecha, v'yasem l'cha shalom.*

May God bless you and keep you.
May God watch over you in kindness.
May God grant you a life of good health,
joy, and peace.